BPM Basics
FOR
DUMMIES®

Software AG Special Edition

by Kiran Garimella,
Michael Lees,
and Bruce Williams

WILEY

Wiley Publishing, Inc.

BPM Basics For Dummies,® Software AG Special Edition

Published by
Wiley Publishing, Inc.
111 River Street
Hoboken, NJ 07030-5774

Copyright © 2008 by Wiley Publishing, Inc., Indianapolis, Indiana

Published by Wiley Publishing, Inc., Indianapolis, Indiana

For general information on our other products and services, please contact our Customer Care Department within the U.S. at 800-762-2974, outside the U.S. at 317-572-3993, or fax 317-572-4002.

ISBN: 978-0-470-28571-8

Manufactured in the United States of America

10 9

WILEY

About the Authors

Dr. Kiran K. Garimella is Vice President of BPM Solutions at Software AG. Previously, he was a Chief Architect and a Chief Information Officer at General Electric, and he has over 18 years of global experience in management consulting, business architecture, and teaching. He is the author of a business novel on Business Process Management, *The Power of Process: Unleashing the Source of Competitive Advantage*, and an active writer of articles and whitepapers, as well as three blogs on BPM and related methodologies. He is a frequent speaker at BPM conferences and related events around the world. He is Six Sigma certified from GE, with project experience in Six Sigma and Lean. Dr. Garimella holds a BS in Chemistry, an MS in Computer Science, and a Ph.D. in Decision and Information Sciences from the Warrington College of Business, University of Florida.

Michael J. Lees is Director of BPM Product Marketing at Software AG, and previously held a similar position at webMethods, Inc. Prior to joining webMethods he was Founder and CEO of the market-leading metadata and knowledge management vendor Cerebra, Inc., which was acquired by webMethods in 2006. He has held senior positions in technology analysis and fund management organizations. Michael is a qualified UK Chartered Accountant (ACA) and has a degree in Business Economics from Durham University, England.

Bruce D. Williams is Senior Vice President and General Manager of the BPM Solutions Group for Software AG. He was previously VP of BPM Solutions for webMethods. In prior business lives, he was the founding principal of Savvi International, a CPI training and consulting firm, and the founding executive of Entrada Software, a PLM company. He previously held management positions with Sybase, Inc. and Ball Aerospace Systems. He has graduate degrees in Engineering Computing and Technical Management from Johns Hopkins University and the University of Colorado, and a BS in Physics also from Colorado. Bruce is coauthor of *Six Sigma For Dummies*, *The Six Sigma Workbook For Dummies*, and *Lean For Dummies*.

Dedications

Kiran Garimella: To my wife Raji, daughters Lillian and Angela, for their patience and encouragement; and to my mother, Dr. Seeta Garimella, for being an inspiration.

Mike Lees: For Ben and Katie, who have yet to understand the phrase, "Daddy has to work" . . . This is what I do!

Bruce Williams: To My Beloved Audrey; it's good to know you're always on my side.

Authors' Acknowledgements

The authors acknowledge Nancy Beckman, Julie Sheridan, Sherry Bussel, and Kevin Iaquinto at Software AG for their technical and administrative assistance in the preparation of this work.

Our special thanks to our colleagues at Cox Communications, especially Bruce Beeco, and also Norman Gottschalk of Lenders First Choice, for pushing us — and the envelope.

We especially thank Roger Burlton at the Process Renewal Group, Peter Fingar of The Greystone Group, Roxanne O'Brasky at the International Society of Six Sigma Professionals, Celia Wolf and Paul Harmon of BPTrends, and Dr. Richard Welke of Georgia State University, for their insight and participation in the development of the global BPM movement.

And we'd like to acknowledge our many BPM friends and colleagues at Software AG, especially Matt Green, Peter Carlson, Reed Wellman, James Crump, Sami Morcos, Susan Ganeshan, Phani Pandrangi, Anthony Coker, Bob Brooks, Russ West, Stewart Loewen, Michael Cupps, William Brown, and Doug Sheeran, whose collective dedication to BPM and process excellence has driven us all to new heights of capability and accomplishment.

Table of Contents

Introduction

*B*usiness Process Management (BPM) was unheard of just a few years ago, but it has burst onto the global scene to become the hottest business and technology management trend of the decade. If you're in any business or industry — public or private — you've probably heard of the movement toward *process,* or about things like *process management* or *process improvement.* You may know about process improvement methods like Lean and Six Sigma or about new technologies like Business Activity Monitoring (BAM) or Service-Oriented Architectures (SOA).

BPM represents a culmination of all the collective experience, thinking, and professional development in business management over the past several decades. It's customer first. It's business focused. It empowers people in all corners of a business to be more successful. It brings people and systems together. BPM is where all the lofty goals and best strategies are coming home to roost.

You stir all these things together and it can start sounding pretty confusing. But really, BPM is very simple. It's a set of methods, tools, and technologies used to design, enact, analyze, and control operational business processes; a process-centric approach for improving performance that combines information technologies with process methodologies.

About This Book

This book helps you understand what BPM is really all about. We wrote it because BPM is so useful and so powerful — and because it is also very accessible. We wrote this book for you — the individual. You may be a business manager, or an Information Technology practitioner, or maybe an ambitious career individual who wants to know what BPM is all about and how to apply it.

BPM Basics For Dummies, Software AG Special Edition is more than just an overview or survey of BPM. It covers both the business management and information technology sides, and delves into the process-centric foundation upon which BPM is built. As a basics book, it is necessarily brief, so you'll want to follow up in some of the areas that are most interesting or important to you.

We wrote this book not only for you to read, but also for you to use as a business reference, to help you while you practice everyday BPM. *BPM Basics For Dummies* should help you establish a sound conceptual basis for understanding BPM, and help you appreciate how BPM is applied to achieve break-through business performance improvement.

This book is:

- ✔ A reference book that's organized into chapters, so you can flip right to what you need

- ✔ A text that addresses the core concepts and practical ideas in BPM

- ✔ A primer for getting started with BPM

- ✔ A step-by-step guide for implementing BPM successfully

- ✔ A compilation of resources that you can go to for additional help or continued education

We use some business management, process improvement, and information technology concepts and language in this book. To get extra smart on some of these aspects, check out *Lean For Dummies* by Natalie Sayer and Bruce Williams; *Six Sigma For Dummies* by Craig Gygi and Bruce Williams, and the *Six Sigma Workbook For Dummies* by Craig Gygi, Bruce Williams, and Terry Gustafson. Also check out *Balanced Scorecard Strategy For Dummies* by Chuck Hannabarger, Rick Buchman, and Peter Economy (all published by Wiley).

Foolish Assumptions

We assume that you have heard something about BPM or process management, and are intrigued about what it can do for you and your business. You want to find out more, for at least one of these reasons:

✔ Your company is considering BPM, and intends to implement it, and you need to understand what it is and how it works.

✔ Your company is implementing BPM now, and you need to know how to use it to improve the performance of your business area.

✔ You're a practitioner of a process improvement methodology like Lean or Six Sigma, and you want to know how these and BPM fit together.

✔ You're a manager, analyst, or practitioner in the IT organization; you know BPM will have a big impact on your future, and you want to know what BPM will mean to you.

✔ You've heard a lot about BPM, and now you want to really understand it!

Whatever the reason you've picked up this book, we're assuming that you're a business or information technology professional, that you recognize the potential in your organization for performance improvement, and that you're ready to be part of the solution.

Icons Used in This Book

In the margins of this book, you will see some helpful little icons that can help you pinpoint particular types of information:

Key points for implementing BPM successfully.

Caution — a risk or pitfall could get you into trouble.

When you see this, it's an indication of a technical detail.

A Remember icon pinpoints the most important ideas in the book. Pay attention when you see this!

Where to Go from Here

This book is organized into chapters on specific topics. You can read it straight through or you can use it as a reference. If you're brand new to BPM, start at the beginning, with Chapter 1. If you're most interested in the technical aspects, start with Chapter 5. Interested in the business and management side? See Chapter 4. Want to know how to implement BPM? Look at Chapter 6. Need to know all the language and lexicon of BPM? See our Glossary in Appendix A.

But no matter where you begin, be sure to read the whole book, because BPM is more than the process, management, and technology pieces; it's a complete and systematic way to look at your business. And besides, it's only 72 pages — you'll get through it in no time!

BPM is a big deal, because it makes a big difference in business performance. BPM can be a very big opportunity for you and your business. We wish you well on your BPM journey. We're here with you, and with this book by your side, you'll have a good start on knowing the way.

Chapter 1

Defining Business Process Management (BPM)

*B*usiness Process Management (BPM) is a set of methods, tools, and technologies used to design, enact, analyze, and control operational business processes. BPM is a process-centric approach for improving performance that combines information technologies with process and governance methodologies. BPM is a collaboration between business people and information technologists to foster effective, agile, and transparent business processes. BPM spans people, systems, functions, businesses, customers, suppliers, and partners.

Like many people, you may find this confusing. What are "operational business processes"? Or what's a "process-centric approach"? And since when do business and IT people "collaborate"? Don't worry — we explain all of this.

BPM combines established and proven process management methods with a new class of enterprise software tools. It's enabled breakthroughs in the speed and agility of how organizations improve business performance. With BPM:

✔ Business managers can more directly measure, respond to, and control all the aspects and elements of their operational processes.

> ✔ Information technology managers can apply their skills and resources more directly on business operations.
>
> ✔ Staff and workers across the organization can better align their efforts and improve personal productivity and performance.
>
> ✔ The enterprise as a whole can more quickly respond to changes and challenges to continuously meet its goals and objectives.

Sound too good to be true? Well, this time, it's true. BPM is quickly changing the landscape of global business.

The Three Dimensions of BPM

BPM is aptly named, because it addresses the comprehensive world of an enterprise across its three core dimensions.

Business: The value dimension

The business dimension is the dimension of value, and of the creation of value for both customers and stakeholders. BPM directly facilitates the goals and objectives of the business enterprise: sustained top-line growth and improved bottom-line performance; increased innovation; improved productivity; enhanced customer loyalty and satisfaction; and elevated levels of staff effectiveness.

BPM brings more capability than ever before to align operational activities with goals and strategies. It focuses enterprise resources and effort on the creation of customer value. BPM also enables a much faster response to change, fostering the agility needed for continuous adaptation.

Process: The transformation dimension

The process dimension creates value through structured activities called processes. Operational processes transform resources and materials into products or services for customers and end consumers. This "transformation" is how a business works; it's the magic elixir of the enterprise. The more effective this transformation, the more successfully you create value.

The applied science of processes and transformation spans the history of modern industrial management — from the quality gurus like Deming, Juran, Shingo, Crosby, and Peters and recently the practices of Lean and Six Sigma. BPM fully incorporates these methodologies, and accelerates them with dramatically enhanced systems of definition, measurement, analysis, and control.

Through BPM, business processes are more effective, more transparent, and more agile. Problems are solved before they become issues. Processes produce fewer errors, and those errors surface faster and are fixed sooner.

Process effectiveness

Effective processes are more consistent, generate less waste, and create greater net value for customers and stakeholders. BPM directly promotes increased process effectiveness through the adaptive automation and coordination of people, information, and systems.

Unlike methods and tools of the past, BPM doesn't impose effectiveness through rigid and unyielding systems of control focused on functional domains. Instead, BPM enables the continuous response and adaptation to real-world and real-time events and conditions.

Process transparency

Transparency is the property of openness and visualization — and it's critical to effective operations. Transparency has long eluded businesses, whose processes are often codified into arcane systems, unintelligible to mere mortals. BPM opens these black boxes and reveals the inner workings of business processes. With BPM, you can directly see all the elements of a process design, including the model, workflows, rules, systems, and participants, as well as its real-time performance, including events and trends. BPM enables business people to directly manipulate the structure and flow of processes and track the outcomes as well as the causes.

Process agility

Of all demands on business operations, perhaps the most pressing is the need for change — the ability to adapt to changing events and circumstances while still maintaining overall productivity and performance. BPM delivers process agility, minimizing the time and effort needed to translate business needs and ideas into action. BPM enables business people to define processes quickly and accurately through process models. It enables them to perform what-if analysis on business scenarios. It empowers them to configure, customize, and change transaction flows by modifying business rules. It directly translates process designs into execution — integrating systems and building applications codelessly and seamlessly. Moreover, the BPM platform comes equipped with technology components that make codeless development and integration fast and easy.

Management: The enabling dimension

Management is the enabling dimension. Management sets people and systems into motion and prods processes into action, in pursuit of the business goals and objectives.

For management, processes are the tools with which they forge business success. Before BPM, constructing and applying these tools spawned an unwieldy mix of enterprise-class automation, many isolated desktop tools, manual methods and techniques, and brute force. With BPM, you can bring together all the systems, methods, tools, and techniques of process development and process management into an architected system, complete with the visibility and controls necessary for steering and tuning. How could you not want that?

The Catalyst: BPM Technology

Business leaders and managers know the fundamental roles of business, process, and management in the enterprise. These have been defined, studied, and improved over a period of decades. Technology, however, has been evolving more rapidly, and recently, significant advancements have changed the game. BPM technology is the new enabler that has taken business, process, and management to new levels. BPM technology is the key ingredient of BPM — it's the catalyst in a new, faster, and more effective business alchemy.

BPM technology is the result of many years of development and application experience; the product of the most current advances in information systems and processing; the pinnacle of all computing architectures, languages, and protocols. BPM technology is a breakthrough, and a new paradigm in flexibility, management, and control of data and information. BPM, as a comprehensive management practice, is the result of combining the technical advancements with established methods and practices of a process-centric business model.

BPM technology includes everything you need to design, enact, analyze, and control operational business processes:

- ✓ **Process Modeling and Design** make it possible for you to quickly and rigorously define processes that span value chains, and to orchestrate the roles and behaviors of all necessary people, systems, and other resources.

- ✓ **Integration** allows you to include any information system, control system, data source, or other technology into business processes. Service-Oriented Architecture (SOA) makes it faster and easier than ever before. Nothing of value need be discarded; everything is reusable.

- ✓ **Composite Application Frameworks** allow you to build and deploy fully-functional Web-based applications *codelessly* and almost instantly.

- ✓ **Execution** directly turns models into real-world action, orchestrating processes in real-time.

- ✓ **Business Activity Monitoring** tracks process performance as it's happening, monitoring many indicators, displaying key process metrics and trends, and predicting future behaviors.

- ✓ **Control** allows you to respond to process events based on circumstances, such as rule changes, notifications, exceptions, and escalations.

BPM: A Model for Success

Because processes represent value chains that often cut across functional departments and even separate businesses, BPM initiates important shifts in business architecture and management practice. BPM orchestrates processes, and that has implications on the ways people communicate. The behaviors are different — and that has implications on roles, job descriptions, and incentives.

BPM & CPI: Birds of a feather

Continuous Process Improvement (CPI) methodologies like Six Sigma and Lean are naturally part of BPM. These time-tested approaches to process optimization are extended in force and range when combined with BPM technology. BPM is the platform that takes CPI to the enterprise level. BPM accelerates the adoption and execution of CPI methodologies, and propagates best practices throughout the enterprise.

BPM sustains the effectiveness of CPI.

BPM is business infrastructure

BPM brings all dimensions of a business together, and enables new levels of participation and collaboration among teams — especially between business staff and IT professionals. BPM promotes quick, incremental improvements while reaching levels of process stability and performance quickly.

BPM is the central discipline — including the tools and the techniques — that connects enterprises and organizations by fostering operational process performance with effectiveness, transparency, and agility.

BPMS: A Suite Deal

There's an "S" that you'll sometimes see on the end of BPM. The "S" in BPMS stands for "Suite."

A BPMS is the suite of BPM technologies — including all the functional modules, technical capabilities, and supporting infrastructure — integrated into a single environment that performs all the BPM technology functions seamlessly. A BPMS is the total package.

Chapter 2

The Business Drivers of BPM

. . . .

. . . .

*W*hy are businesses across the globe adopting BPM practices and technologies? Because BPM addresses each of today's most significant business drivers.

The Business Imperatives

The pressures on organizations and enterprises around the world are increasing. Markets are crowded; margins are squeezed. New challenges pop up seemingly overnight on all fronts. Believe it or not, BPM can help you improve your offerings in all of the following categories:

✔ **Globalization:** Companies are going further to find advantages in cost, quality, and innovation. Successful business now requires seamless integration of processes and the instant exchange of information on a planetary scale. Fonterra, the largest global exporter of dairy products, uses BPM to streamline its supply chain operations.

✔ **Commoditization:** In mature, commoditized markets, competing products and services are nearly indistinguishable to the consumer, forcing providers to differentiate along a single factor, such as price. Companies in commodity markets must achieve new levels of efficiency and cost control in order to survive, and they must invest in innovation in order to grow. In the highly commoditized consumer lending industry, U.S. banks are using BPM to close lending processes faster.

✔ **Productivity:** You have to produce more, and generate more value, with fewer resources and in less time. Continuously. Toyota became the world's largest automotive company with this mantra. Lean is now the global framework for implementing the Toyota Production System and achieving continuous improvement in productivity. Companies everywhere are steadily driving for improved productivity.

✔ **Innovation:** Perhaps the business word of the decade, "innovation" is exhaustively attached to invention, breakthrough, excitement, and everything new. But that's just the product marketing definition of innovation. Business innovation is much more. While mostly associated with products, innovation also applies to services, business and manufacturing processes, development, store design, business models, and even packaging.

✔ **Speed:** You hear it every day: somebody suddenly introduced a new product or service, and took a big share of the market from an established firm. Its brand, reach, and resources couldn't protect it from the more nimble newbie — it couldn't move fast enough.

✔ **Compliance:** Regulatory and governance requirements are drowning companies in bureaucratic exercises that drain value. The cost of regulatory compliance has been growing, but is growing even more quickly in IT as companies attempt to reduce the overall cost of compliance by automating processes and reporting.

✔ **Information overload:** The world is now data rich, but information starved. People struggle with gleaning true intelligence from the vast stores of data and information. Market and customer intelligence are necessary weapons in the Age of Information.

✔ **The changing nature of people and work:** In the era of the knowledge worker and the transition to intellectual capital, the nature of work has changed. Many work environments are now characterized by flexible time, telecommuting, collaboration, social networks, and increasing dependence on information and communications technology. Reaching higher levels of productivity and performance requires new approaches.

✔ **Customer first:** You'd better put the customer first, because if you don't, you can be certain that they won't put you first. Or second. Or even on the list. Customers have more choices, more freedoms, and a much more developed sense of needs, wants, and desires than ever before. Customers are savvy, and can quickly spot poor quality and service. Over half of all major global businesses now use Balanced Scorecards or Net Promoter Scores to track the influencers on customer satisfaction.

The cost of low customer loyalty is high; the cost of customer defection is astronomical.

✔ **And there's more:** This list is by no means exhaustive. It's representative of the broad nature of challenges besetting enterprises and institutions of all types and sizes around the world.

BPM Business Drivers

Four core business drivers are motivating the adoption of BPM.

✔ **Improving a process or sub-process:** Companies implement BPM as a means for improving selected processes. Typically, these are not complete process frameworks or value chains, but sub-processes within a value chain. In these cases, BPM offers a faster time to a solution. This also serves as a pilot to a first experience with BPM.

✔ **BPM(S) for CPI:** Because of the synergistic relationship between BPM and Continuous Process Improvement methodologies like Lean, Six Sigma, SCOR, TQM, and so on, many companies who have embarked on a CPI initiative implement a BPMS as the technology companion and enabler to their CPI program.

✔ **BPM for SOA:** Many IT organizations have adopted Service-Oriented Architectures (SOA) and are exposing services for next-generation integration. BPM directly leverages SOA, and together the combined BPMS (suite) is a higher-value system.

 ✔ **Business Transformation:** BPM, as the combination of BPM technology and CPI methods, represents the most complete, comprehensive, and holistic framework for enacting strategic business transformation.

BPM: Something for Everyone

The value propositions of BPM are extensive. All corners of the enterprise can reap benefits from BPM. Here are just a few:

 ✔ **Automation:** Increased productivity, consistency, reduction in errors, maximized customer satisfaction, and compliance.

 ✔ **Agility:** Faster response times to issues, faster time to develop solutions, faster turnaround time.

 ✔ **Flexibility:** Combining the scale, scope, and capacity of legacy information systems with the agility, flexibility, and innovation of modern technologies such as Web 2.0; and enhancing an information platform with the tools and techniques of CPI, Balanced Scorecards, methodology, governance, frameworks, and metadata.

 ✔ **Visibility:** Tracing individual business transactions (even in real-time) throughout the entire process, drilling down into sub-processes, zooming up to the parent processes, and seeing the process through the perspective of any particular role.

 ✔ **Collaboration:** Alignment and participation, especially between IT and business.

 ✔ **Governance:** A strong model of management control and change that builds confidence in customers, partners, suppliers, regulators, and shareholders. BPM ensures policies of use and re-use are followed, and provides oversight to tasks and the flow of work.

Chapter 3

The Functional Goals of BPM

*W*hen you say BPM, what does that mean in terms of what people actually do? This chapter is a description of the functional capabilities of BPM, how the inner workings relate to one other, and how people use BPM to improve business performance. (The technology architecture of BPM is described in Chapter 5.)

What Does BPM Do?

BPM is a broad discipline, but it has a specific functional purpose. And, of course, the BPM technology components have precise specifications. How do these all come together? Here's a list that explains:

 ✔ **Process-Centricity:** BPM unifies business and IT activities and coordinates the actions and behaviors of people and systems around the common context of business processes. Using standard process modeling conventions and notations, an operations manager, for example, sees the process from a business perspective, while the IT manager sees the systems and information elements.

✔ **Business/IT Alignment:** BPM facilitates the direct collaboration and joint responsibility of business and IT professionals in developing, implementing, and optimizing operational business processes. The same process model, for example, provides a business perspective for the business analyst and a systems perspective for the systems analyst.

✔ **Continuous Process Improvement:** BPM implements the management and behavioral methods and tools of Continuous Process Improvement (CPI). For example, each functional module of a BPMS supports one or more of the DMAIC phases of Six Sigma, and Business Activity Monitoring allows you to monitor Six Sigma metrics for your processes.

✔ **Composition of Solutions:** BPM facilitates the rapid design, assembly, and deployment of complete business processes. A developer attaches IT systems and services to the same process model designed by the business analyst. A complete set of connectors and codeless tools makes the development of solutions even faster.

✔ **Transparency:** BPM provides real-time, cross-functional visibility into operational processes and a common understanding of activities for all participants. An operations manager, for example, can view running business processes and their business metrics in real time, and an IT manager can see the supporting systems' availability and performance.

✔ **Leave and Layer:** BPM directly incorporates existing information systems and assets and coordinates their use within a process "layer" accessible to business managers. A comprehensive set of system adapters and "business-to-business" (B2B) tools allows you to re-use any of your existing IT applications. Users see one interface in front of many systems. And the BPM dashboards present a unified business façade to business users.

Each of these functional components of BPM adds value to multiple aspects of business performance, such as effectiveness, transparency, and agility.

Process Effectiveness

BPM assumes the paradigm of managing business activities through a framework of operational processes. The term business process may sound loose, but don't be misled; it is a precise term.

A *business process* is the set of all formally coordinated tasks and activities, conducted by both people and equipment, which leads to accomplishing a specific organizational objective. An example of a business process is order fulfillment. The act of a customer placing an order initiates a process to record the order, approve their credit, and trigger the production and delivery.

BPM endeavors to maximize the effectiveness of business processes, by:

- Determining the optimal process for the current conditions
- Making the process operate as effectively as possible
- Enabling decisions and controls for ongoing effectiveness

Optimization

You need to find out what's happening in your business as it's happening, and how potential changes can impact your business.

Real-time monitoring

BPM provides visibility into the state of current processes, and extracts the key metrics that are important to how that process affects the business. This way, you can judge how effective your processes are now, and then design processes that will improve performance against these metrics. For example, you might view the logistics process across your entire global supply chain. You would see status, run-charts, and red flags showing where shipments are delayed. Your BPM platform would send automatic escalations to troubleshooters. You would receive follow-up information that notifies you when shipments are moving again. Your customers would be automatically notified about delays.

'What-if' analysis

With BPM, you can simulate the performance of processes before you implement them. Experiment with different paths, resource levels, rules, and more, asking "what if. . . ?" about how the process could work best. For example, you could simulate the addition of staff in order processing to see what impact such additions would make to the overall performance.

Automation

With BPM, you can automate the execution of many process tasks that may have previously been handled manually. You can combine new and existing services to do this. For tasks that still require manual handling, BPM will coordinate the workflow and direct action by notifying people and presenting them the information they need to perform their work. If the customer service manager needs to review a high-value order, BPM sends a notification via e-mail or to a task inbox in the process workspace.

Control and decision making

BPM gives business managers direct control over certain change and control points in how the information systems facilitate process management. Managers have unimpeded access to data about process performance. Business users participate both in the specification of the initial process defi- nition and also in changes to keep it continuously optimized. Business managers also have direct control of the rules and policies that govern process behaviors. For more on how this works, see Chapter 5.

Sharing control isn't loss of control. IT systems managers can rest assured that BPM provides the governance necessary to ensure business managers implement changes properly.

Process Transparency

Business processes shouldn't be black boxes. BPM provides visibility through modeling and monitoring capabilities.

What you model is what you run

Models are usually just that. You don't actually drive a model car, or move into a model home. Models are representations, and what you experience later is something different. Sometimes, what you experience is *very* different, and when you work with complex systems like operational business processes, it's often *too* different.

But what if the model actually *became* reality? What if the model and the real thing were directly connected and what you modeled was what actually ran? In BPM, what you model is what you run (WYMIWYR).

With BPM, the model isn't just the design — it actually becomes the engine that runs the process. No translations, no muddled interpretations of requirements or design documents. Doing things this way is far faster and much more accurate than the way it's been done before.

In traditional development environments, you must use multiple tools and create different models at each stage of your development life cycle. This gives rise to multiple interpretations and inconsistencies. But BPM gives you a unified design environment that avoids this problem. What you model is what you run.

Process monitoring and analysis

We promise not to make another acronym about it, but it's an old adage: *what you measure is what you manage.* And the converse is true, too: you can't manage what you don't measure. If you can't sense it, you can't respond.

BPM allows you to see processes as they execute, and to determine how the business transactions that flow through the processes affect your key business metrics. BPM provides the tools not just to react and respond, but also to manage impending threats and opportunities proactively. BPM delivers information that helps uncover the root causes of problems and provides actionable, objective feedback as to how the process can be improved.

Sensing deterioration in the performance of your business requires you to understand what your "normal" operating state is. But "normal" varies depending on time and events. You can use BPM technologies to sense deterioration from what is statistically normal for the current circumstances, rather than relying on abstract thresholds or long-term averages. For example, the number of orders an online toy store receives tend to be greater in December. Operations managers don't want to compare December sales volume to October or November. They want it compared to the prior December, and they want to be alerted if orders deviate significantly from the expected level for December.

How about them processes?

Business processes are complex assemblies of models, rules, data, logic, services, and lots more. The structured collection of information that describes all these pieces and how they work together is called *metadata*. BPM uses metadata to keep everything straight. (For more on metadata, see Chapter 5.)

An architecture of reusable components means you have many more moving parts in your business. With different people controlling and changing different components, it can be a challenge to maintain a clear picture of how all of the moving parts interact. Metadata allows you to store the descriptions of all of these pieces and the relationships between them in a central repository. You need this view of what's going on to manage all the assemblies and dependencies.

Process Agility

Process effectiveness and transparency are powerful enough, but with BPM, you also have process agility. BPM directly enables change, both by streamlining existing processes and developing new ones.

Communication and collaboration

The greatest barrier to change is communication. BPM lowers this barrier by increasing the direct and immediate lines of

communications and collaboration among all process participants. BPM enables the process team to:

✔ Agree on the metrics of business process performance

✔ Share process models and common business semantics

✔ Clearly communicate about the tasks to be performed

And this goes beyond your four walls (that's just a metaphor,
anyway — it's been a long time since a business was contained
in one place!). BPM allows you to extend your reach into
processes beyond the boundaries of your business, allowing
you to effectively collaborate with your customers, partners,
and suppliers.

Rapid development

BPM is much faster than anything you've experienced before.
It allows you to sense change when it happens, interpret the
impact of that change, and develop a shared understanding
of how the business should respond. It also allows you to
develop and deploy solutions faster than is currently possible.

With BPM, you:

✔ Have a central point of change in the infrastructure for
process and rule logic (the process model)

✔ Minimize the amount of code that must be developed and
maximize the reuse of existing capabilities

✔ Expose existing functionality as discrete reusable services that can be graphically assembled into new applications and processes

✔ Share the burden of design and change outside of the
IT group

✔ Quickly simulate the operation of new processes prior to
deployment

Productive Workspaces

People working in and around formal business processes are often forced to interact with multiple existing systems, including packaged applications. Coordinating this hodge-podge has become a productivity-draining part of our everyday world. Packaged applications and fixed systems can't readily be customized to the individual needs of any particular person. The result? People switch back and forth between many systems and applications, and they have to figure out how to make it all work for them.

With BPM, you abstract the process worker from the complexity of different systems and align the work they have to do and the tools they need through a single, personalized process environment.

The practices of CPI and the technologies of BPM make this possible. Process workers are more productive. People like the look and feel. Instead of users changing their work style to suit the applications, the new process environment adapts itself to how people work productively.

For example, in a typical order-entry process, a clerk would have to move between their e-mail, where they were first notified, and the different sales systems to record different parts of the order, as well as the finance system to record the credit transaction and finally the ERP system to check stock levels. With BPM, the clerk would simply see a single view that presents all of the entry fields and notifications needed to complete the order. Each of the existing systems would be updated in the background, but this would not be the concern of the order-entry clerk.

Chapter 4

The Business, Process, and Management Architectures of BPM

. . . .

In This Chapter

▶ Adjusting your architectures for business, process, and management

▶ Appreciating that these architectures are critical to the success of your BPM initiative

▶ Understanding how each architecture is part of BPM

. . . .

*W*ith BPM, you have the ability to develop, deploy, and change business processes faster than ever. However, technology alone doesn't translate business needs into sustainable business advantage. You must plan the architecture of your business, processes, and management. Because of the capabilities of BPM technology, you are more obligated than ever to have a comprehensive enterprise architecture in place. Without it, you risk going in the wrong direction, quickly solving the wrong problems, or just chasing your tail.

Many Architectures in One

An enterprise of any size or any type, in any industry, anywhere in the world, has an overall framework or design to it in order to describe and manage how it works. Business Process Management is a process-centric way of doing business, and it requires you to adjust your enterprise frameworks and your enterprise architecture accordingly. When adopting BPM, think of your enterprise architecture as consisting of four sub-architectures. The technology architecture is addressed in detail in Chapter 5. In this chapter, we address the other three:

- ✔ **Business architecture:** The overall structure of the organization, designed to apply strategies that meet the goals and objectives of its customers and stakeholders

- ✔ **Process architecture:** The methods, practices, and procedures by which the people in the enterprise transform available resources and capital to add value for the customers and stakeholders

- ✔ **Management architecture:** How the actions and behaviors of people and systems, as well as the flow of information over time, are directed in exercising the processes to achieve the business goals

BPM is a business *system*, and it includes the technology architecture described in Chapter 5 in concert with the preceding architectures. Use them to address the business drivers described in Chapter 2 and you will have a more nimble, adaptive, and successful enterprise.

The BPM Business Architecture

A business architecture is the design representation of how an enterprise defines itself in terms of its role and purpose, and how it defines the way it creates value. Every enterprise defines its high-level business goals, and creates an organizational structure, including a functional decomposition into operating units, as a basic structure for meeting its goals. The enterprise develops relationships across those units, and determines how it will relate with its customers, shareholders, and stakeholders. It knows its principles and practices, and develops a distinctive culture and language as well as habits in response to opportunities and challenges. Think about your enterprise and how your business architecture is structured.

Process-centric organizations

For most of the industrial age, enterprises have been organized as a collection of common tasks or functions, such as design, finance, manufacturing, operations, and so on. The prevailing wisdom was that overwhelming economies of scale are afforded by such aggregations. In the latter part of the 20th century, new organizational structures emerged, including *product-line* (where all the functions for a single product are collected), and *matrix* (where expertise from functional organizations is brought in and assigned to projects). More recently, Lean practices have further evolved these models into business architectures that align people, work, and capital to the processes that create customer value.

Business Process Management calls on the organization to adjust its business architecture to directly foster value-creating business processes. The process-driven organization treats these business processes as a portfolio of valuable corporate assets. BPM techniques are used to explicitly define and execute processes in a manner that creates significant benefits.

Redefining roles

It's not easy to modify functional alignments and structures, but BPM asks you to create new roles that cut across functional stovepipes to support the process-centric business. Some of these roles are:

- **Chief process officer:** The executive responsible for defining and enabling the enterprise process architecture, who fosters the process-centric business culture, including skills, systems, and behaviors.

- **Process architect:** The individual who designs and constructs models and frameworks for the core and enabling business processes, including workflows, Key Process Indicators (KPIs), and control plans.

- **Business process owners:** Individuals responsible and accountable for the performance of end-to-end processes.

- **Process engineers**: Individuals who build run-time business processes, including the composition of orchestrated services, composite applications, and systems of measurement, notification, and control.

- **Process analyst** (process psychiatrist): The expert who defines what events should be monitored, diagnoses process problems, and prescribes performance solutions.

- **Process performer** (or process member, process worker): Someone who not only works inside a process, but understands how he fits within an extended value stream.

These roles don't typically describe new headcount. These are new roles for people who already know your business.

Being a process owner

The most important of all roles in a process-centric business is the *process owner* — the individual who designs and coordinates the assembly and participation of all the functions and work activities at all levels within a process. The process owner typically is a business person with the authority or ability to make changes in the process who oversees the entire process life cycle to ensure its performance and effectiveness. The process owner is responsible for the process measurement and feedback systems, process documentation, and the training of the process performers within its structure and conduct. The process owner is also the person ultimately responsible for process improvement.

Working in a process-centric world

A *process participant* is a member of a global stream of people, systems, and technology — all coming together to create value for some customer purpose. Everyone in these participative roles is responsible not only for doing his direct functional jobs — for which he's been highly trained and educated — but also for understanding how his role fits in the bigger picture.

The process participant is aware of his position in the value stream and how his own job affects the people before and after him. Ultimately, through BPM process modeling, the process participant knows precisely how he creates value. BPM workflows help guide him; real-time monitoring provides feedback to him; and BPM control systems help him take action when things are going wrong.

Many business processes were designed long ago for situations and applications that have since changed. Unfortunately, most people working in those processes rarely see the change and ask, "Why are we doing it this way? Can't we do it better?" But the BPM-enabled worker sees processes more clearly, is able to analyze and understand them, and participates directly in making improvements.

Connecting strategy and operations

Process-centric organizations leverage their process frameworks to connect business strategy and departmental operations. You can map strategic intent to performance metrics through a process-based value map. BPM connects methods like Economic Value Added and measures such as the Balanced Scorecard with operational process metrics.

BPM business infrastructure

Within your business architecture is a set of infrastructural elements that you adjust and tune to foster and facilitate successful process-centric behaviors and performance.

Leading and the Leadership Team

As with anything worth doing, BPM requires leadership — to set the vision, effect the change, and stay the course. BPM leadership comes from the enterprise leadership team as well as from within each member of the organization:

- ✔ The Leadership Team articulates the strategic imperative for change, communicates the vision for a process-centric organization and the approach for a continuously-improving enterprise, authorizes structural adjustments, and trumpets the results.

- ✔ Everyone is authorized, empowered, and compelled to measure and analyze performance, participate in the design and implementation of new ways of working, and continuously improve performance outcomes.

Counting the beans: Financial performance

The BPM business architecture ensures that both process performance and process improvements are quantified in terms of financial results. You train both the accounting people and the process teams on how to instrument processes and improvement projects for net value creation. Figure 4-1 shows the top-level financial equation against which all projects are measured.

BPM shines because it not only maximizes the gross value through the development of new capabilities, but it does it with minimized cost, time, and waste.

$$V_{net} = V_{new} - [Cost + Time + Waste]$$

where

V_{net} the net value produced by the project or process

V_{new} the total new value produced

Cost   the total cost of the new process and system

Time   the operational cycle time or development time

Waste   unused or discarded systems or capabilities

Figure 4-1: Quantifying financial results.

Life's more than numbers — the balanced view

Everyone knows that numbers are only one of several sets of indicators that reflect the true health and status of the organization. In fact, financial performance alone is a wholly inadequate guide for evaluating the broad spectrum of customers, employees, suppliers, and distributors as well as the processes and technologies that enable the modern enterprise.

The Balanced Scorecard is a widely-used framework for evaluating an organization along the lines of four major perspectives. One is financial, of course. The others are: customer, process, and learning. Simple and easy to understand, the Balanced Scorecard has been applied in some form as a standard in over half the world's corporations.

Facilitating behavior: HR and training

BPM means new skills. It also means different titles and job descriptions. And new incentives and compensation tied to both quantitative and qualitative measures of process orientation, process improvement, and process performance. Because the introduction of BPM is a new direction, it also means change management.

Training regimens for process design and improvement in BPM are borrowed directly from the Six Sigma and Lean communities. If you already know Lean and Six Sigma, you're well on your way to understanding BPM.

Set up a formal education and training regimen that ensures your process-focused role players are fully capable, and that your technical staff is versed in both the programmatic and technical elements of BPM.

Don't expect business people to become skilled process workers overnight. Process maps and process flow diagrams are foreign to most business folks and take time to understand.

The IT organization for BPM

The changes needed to develop a BPM enterprise are most pronounced in the IT organization, where the functional world of application development and sustaining support is turned over to a collaborative business world of process engineering, application assembly, and business optimization.

Facilitating business participation

BPM represents a sea-change in the organizational alignment of the enterprise IT function. IT is no longer hidden from view and sequestered in a world of arcane computer code. Business people and IT practitioners work collaboratively, with tools like process modelers, codeless application assemblers, and service orchestrators. IT reorganizes itself to support an embedded business process facilitation capability.

The CIO is becoming the CPO

The Information Technology function is splitting in two. At one level, it is pure infrastructure management: tactical, standardized, cost-driven. But at the other level, by using BPM, IT is becoming a strategic enabler of process effectiveness. With this change, IT leadership evolves into a process leadership: The Chief Information Officer becomes the Chief Process Officer.

IT practitioners are becoming process engineers

Because BPM enables shifting the bulk of IT effort from sustaining support to solutions development, and because solutions are composed of orchestrated services, IT staff (and particularly business analysts) elevate their roles from IT practitioners to process engineers.

Most IT shops have many "code-heads" who just want to write computer code. Unless you're a software development company, this isn't your core competence. Over time, train your IT developers to become more process-centric, and enable some of your developers to become process engineers.

Integration competency

Because BPM is naturally integrative of people, process, and technology, it requires a comprehensive and holistic approach to integration. This requires a discipline of integration and a set of business and technical skills to effectively build and maintain process-centric business solutions. You need to:

- Understand where the people, process, and technology assets of the enterprise reside and how they're accessed.

- Make available the repository of standard and reusable connectors, interfaces, source code, and other information integration components, and make them accessible to process engineers and other service creators.

- Exploit patterns of how people access data, information, applications, and services in the integration architecture.

- Consult with the company's IT community, providing expertise on the use of integration tools and techniques.

An Integration Competency Center can follow a centralized model, a federated model, or an engagement model.

The BPM Center of Excellence

Best practices in BPM can be collected and disseminated through what's called a *Center of Excellence* (CoE) — a place for people and information on all things BPM. A BPM CoE establishes standards and methods for implementing projects; helps scope and prioritize projects; identifies roles and staffing for projects, and ensures skills and training; and ensures project and process governance.

The BPM Process Architecture

A *process architecture* is the written or diagrammatic representation of the value chains and business processes that operate across an enterprise. It includes both the core operating processes and enabling management support processes. A process architecture clearly demonstrates where value is created and how operational processes are related and aligned to the strategies and goals of the organization.

In general, a process architecture depicts *orchestrated* processes — processes that are structured, repeatable, and can be automated, and also can be characterized, measured, and analyzed. The order-entry process described in Chapter 3 is an example of an orchestrated process. Note that much of the activity in an enterprise is *ad-hoc;* it occurs outside the bounds of orchestration. Ad-hoc process management is a critical future element of BPM.

The process framework

Processes are one of two types: *core* (direct) and *enabling* (indirect). Core and enabling processes can be assembled into larger value chains known as *process frameworks.* Core process frameworks include customer value-stream processes like new product introduction, order-to-cash, and procure-to-pay. Enabling process frameworks include employee on-boarding and resource management. Collectively, process frameworks make up the process architecture, and include all processes used by the enterprise.

Process methodologies

To construct the process frameworks and align processes in the process architecture, you must follow a methodology. A process methodology is a blueprint for both characterizing and optimizing business processes. Process methodologies are often known also as process *improvement* methodologies because improving process performance is so popular — and desirable. But process methodologies like SCOR, Lean, and Six Sigma do more: They not only set the basis for defining and improving processes, they also provide the comprehensive approach for tying people, process, and technology performance into the creation of value.

Process methodologies are not all the same, and they're not one-size-fits-all. Selecting the process methodology to accompany your BPM initiative is a critically important task. You must fit the methodology to the type, size, condition, and cultural elements of your enterprise.

The process life-cycle

The goal for any process is to be steady and continuously in a state of peak performance. To get there, and stay there, process managers embark on projects that take the process through analysis and improvement. The states of change through which a process is transitioned from one performing condition to the next are known as the *process life-cycle.*

The process life-cycle is defined by a combination of industry conditions and your process methodology. Different process methodologies, such as CMMI, IDEAL, Lean, and Six Sigma, have their own set of life cycle phases.

The Management Architecture for BPM

Management's role is to set everything in motion. Within the framework of the business architecture, management's role is to direct the actions and behaviors of people and systems, as well as the flow of information over time — all the while operating and adjusting the processes to achieve the business goals. The BPM management architecture includes project management, process management, and process improvement.

BPM project management

A BPM project is a new kind of business project. It's part process and part technology. Sometimes it's an improvement project, and sometimes it's a complete redesign. The scope can be as small as a single process or as large as an entire value stream. A BPM project is fast, but not loose. Unlike a typical business program or software development project, BPM projects are implemented iteratively, in short cycle times.

Planning

BPM project planning requires you to follow a process methodology, such as Lean, Six Sigma, or SCOR. Project objectives, staffing, scoping, milestones, and deliverables then follow from the methodology. Typical BPM projects take from as little as a few days to as long as several months.

Analysis and design

Once scoped, BPM projects begin by characterizing the as-is process baseline. The current state is measured and validated, forming the baseline conditions against which progress and improvements are compared.

The team designs and deploys not what it considers to be the ideal state, but the next future state — the next best thing. This approach is a critical distinction and a departure from classical development, which seeks to construct the ideal state. In this way, the agility and platform for BPM makes continuous improvement possible.

Process design is a facilitated activity, involving all classes of process participants in sessions that may consume up to one-third of the project schedule.

To optimize your design, you may find it necessary to analyze process models via simulation. Process simulation is an advanced discipline that BPM makes easier.

Composition and deployment

Developing automated business processes requires the composition of services that perform the functions and stimulate the actions to be taken by people and systems per the process model. This composition isn't anything like historical application development: the schedule is shorter, review cycles are faster, and the documentation is self-generating.

The rules governing business actions in a running process are "externalized" from the process execution engine into what's known as a *rules engine*. These rules are accessible at any time to business managers who can modify them without changing business logic. For more on how this works, see Chapter 5.

Process management

Once a process is performing within specifications, your goal is to keep it there — indefinitely (until the next improvement is warranted). Bank of America famously stated that their goal is not to complete a million successful transactions, but instead to complete one successful transaction — and then repeat it a million times. That's process management.

Once deployed, a process model is orchestrated by a runtime engine, which facilitates the timely and consistent execution of the services and provides the value-added transformation of inputs and information to outputs and results. Process performance is measured in real-time and the deployed process is monitored for performance to specifications. Volume, velocity, and errors are tracked and recorded.

Whenever a process experiences an out-of-limits condition, Business Activity Monitoring (BAM) detects the event and takes action. The actions, specified in the process model, can range from the custom notifications of individuals (by display, pager, text message, and so on) to extensive automated system interactions. In BPM, process managers can quickly search the root cause of the problem and take action.

The power of BAM can't be overstated. BAM provides process managers unequaled visibility and transparency into events and conditions as they happen, in real-time.

Process improvement

All processes degrade over time. Eventually, wear and tear — and other common and special-cause variations — get the best of them. In other cases, new business needs or new technologies arise. Even a process running perfectly a million times a day may become obsolete.

Process improvement methodologies like Lean and Six Sigma can both correct defects in processes and improve their effectiveness. CPI methods are a core part of BPM.

Chapter 5

The Technology Architecture of BPM

*B*PM provides the most comprehensive and flexible process-centric approach to operational business infrastructure ever devised. The technology architecture compliments the business, process, and management architectures (see Chapter 4) to meet business needs and goals.

The technology architecture of BPM includes the set of component technologies that combine to support the functional goals and business drivers. Specifically, the architecture:

✔ Cost-effectively supports rapid change and continuous innovation

✔ Continuously aligns IT resources with business objectives

✔ Allows existing IT assets to be managed as a portfolio for maximum efficiency and productivity

✔ Allows shared responsibility for the creation and change of process-centric applications between the business and IT

BPM Technology Architecture

The major components of the technical architecture include:

✔ **The Unified Workspace:** User interfaces, monitoring and dashboards, and task inboxes

✔ **The Execution Environment:** Business rules engine, the process engine, and the analytics engine

✔ **The Simulation Engine**

✔ **The Process Design Toolbox:** Process modeling, rule definition, KPI definition, process development, and user interface design

✔ **The Metadata Repository:** The "container" for process asset descriptions, relationships, and policies

✔ **Web Service Adapters and New Services Development Environment:** Provides connections to existing functionality and tools for creation of new services

Figure 5-1 is a visual depiction of the main architectural components of BPM and how they relate to each other.

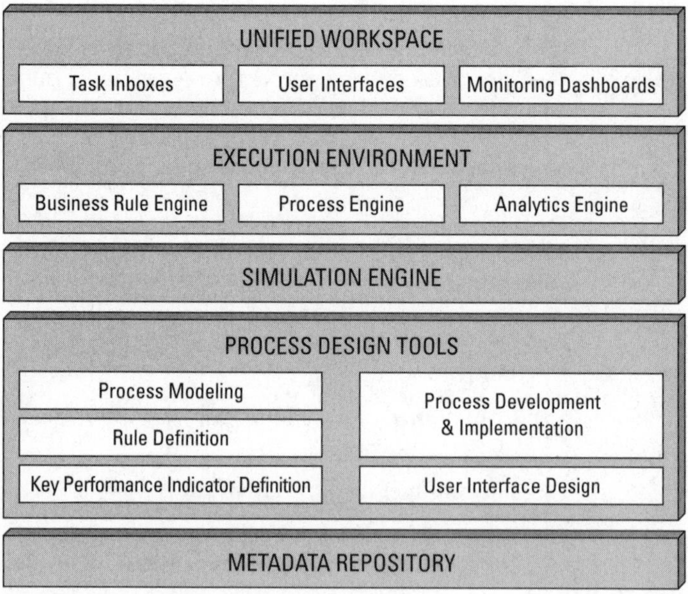

UNIFIED WORKSPACE

Task Inboxes	User Interfaces	Monitoring Dashboards

EXECUTION ENVIRONMENT

Business Rule Engine	Process Engine	Analytics Engine

SIMULATION ENGINE

PROCESS DESIGN TOOLS

Process Modeling	Process Development & Implementation
Rule Definition	
Key Performance Indicator Definition	User Interface Design

METADATA REPOSITORY

Figure 5-1: The BPM technology architecture.

Middleware: The Physical Glue

Middleware is the software that facilitates communications and mobility of data between different IT applications. BPM leverages functionality from across the applications and data landscape using middleware in two ways:

1. Invoke applications over Application Program Interfaces (APIs) using custom code. This approach is the old way. It hard-wires business processes into the underlying applications, making it difficult to reconfigure and improve processes over time. This approach has been used in the past, but it doesn't support the BPM drivers of agility, flexibility, IT productivity, and business empowerment.

2. Use standard interfaces called *adapters* to communicate with systems — regardless of the platform or geographical location of those systems. This approach overcomes the brittle, point-to-point nature of custom interfaces. Adapters can be applied to internal applications (via Enterprise Application Integration or EAI) or those of partner organizations (via Business-to-Business connections, known as B2B).

With the recent advent of Service-Oriented Architecture (SOA), integration solutions are now evolving into what's called Enterprise Service Bus (ESB) solutions. ESBs use standard Web service interfaces and a bus topography to wrap existing IT assets as Web services to be called by the process execution environment (see Figure 5-2).

BPM architectures use an ESB for their underlying integration, maximizing flexibility and scalability, thus ensuring the benefits of SOA can be fully realized.

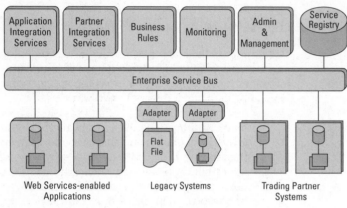

Figure 5-2: The Enterprise Service Bus architecture

Metadata: The Logical Glue

Metadata is "data about data" — information about your data. Metadata is the logical architecture — the roadmap or reference guide that helps you and your systems to know where to go to get information services and processes. Metadata is critical to facilitating discovery, interpretation, and impact analysis in BPM. It describes services, including their attributes and even relationships to other metadata.

Metadata is kept in a *controlled repository* — a centralized library for storing information about all the parts and pieces (known as *assets*) of process designs, including Web services, rule services, process models, documents, and more. The repository is used both to source components for reuse in the assembly of new processes and to find completed sub-process models that can be reused in the development of other processes.

There's more. When assets are developed and stored in a BPMS code versioning system (CVS), fixed properties (role, user, system, service, WSDL, and so on) are defined for those assets and are also stored as metadata.

Metadata repositories come with a search capability that allows you to find all these assets using what's called *rich-attribute*-based search techniques — it's like using a search engine for your process assets. Many repositories also allow

users to *tag* assets with custom metadata by providing simple
user interfaces for attaching words to asset files.

Many metadata repositories now use *semantic technologies* to
organize the metadata. These technologies are based on industry standards such as the Resource Description Framework
(RDF) and the Web Ontology Language (called OWL). These
semantic technologies let you put in full descriptions of components and define the relationships between metadata elements. They also help you to maintain complex relationships
between components and keep track of the many dependencies between them — particularly when things change or new
assets are added. For example, semantic technology notifies a
developer to modify a process when a Web service that is
used by that process has its output format changed.

Unified Modeling

For business and technical people to work together modeling
new processes, BPM provides a comprehensive set of capabilities in a single unified development environment. This unified
modeling environment helps them collaborate on process
modeling, Key Performance Indicator (KPI) definition, composite application design, and the definition of business rules
and task routing rules. An increasing number of these tools
are built on standard design and development platforms such
as Eclipse, allowing support for users with a variety of skill
levels, and enabling the use of drag-and-drop capabilities,
source code control, versioning, debugging, and more.

Defining processes and designing workflows

The process design tool allows business analysts to design
and document executable processes. They can also define the
KPIs used as measures of the process. As shown in Figure 5-3,
process design tools are graphical, and usually allow process
developers to use the drag-and-drop technique.

Development tools usually produce process descriptions in
a standard modeling notation, such as the BPMN or XPDL.
This permits better understanding and communication
between developers.

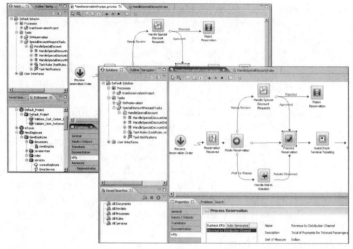

Figure 5-3: A graphical process design tool. There are views for both the technical developer (top) and the business user.

However, certain elements can't be modeled in an executable form within the tool. In cases such as this, most tools allow for the documentation of requirements around the process for clear communication to process developers.

Routing rules for workflow range from the simple to the complex. A simple rule might be:

> Always route bug fix requests to Joe.

More complex rules are based on events that occur during process run-time, such as:

> When customer complaints come in from companies that exceeded $1M in sales in the past year, send them to VP Customer Service.

Most BPM tools also integrate processes with calendar tools like Microsoft Outlook; or they may have the ability to define a calendar directly in the tool itself. With calendars, you can route workflows more intelligently, based on whether an individual is available to perform a particular task or whether a business unit in a particular geography is open for business.

Developing processes

Process design tools reveal all the important technical details you need to implement process steps using existing services that have been built and hosted in the ESB or standard Web Services environment. Developers build processes working from the same process model defined by the business people, using the corresponding documentation they provide. Developers edit the model or expand on steps to build them out as complete sub-processes. They add in other technical details, such as information on services, data formats, transformation, mapping, logging, security, and availability.

Defining business rules

Business rules are the policies and procedures that automate decision points within a business process. Historically, business rules were built into the logic and code of applications like ERP. This made accessing and changing them difficult, because the business manager responsible for the rule couldn't do it without time-consuming and extensive IT support. A compelling and valuable part of BPM is that these rules are *externalized* out of the application code and managed separately in *rules engines* using interfaces that are accessible to the business managers.

BPM technology makes extensive use of rules. Rules govern workflow routing and alert managers of events. For example:

> If average order volume trends up by more
> than two standard deviations, send an alert
> to the VP of Finance.

Business rules can also make decisions automatically:

> If the loan applicant is an existing customer,
> and their credit score is above 760 and loan
> amount is less than $20,000, then automati-
> cally approve the loan.

Authorized users can change process rules in two ways: They can directly edit the rules within a production environment, or edit rules within a development environment and then promote them through the normal release cycle. This agility enables users to react to events and changes in the business environment without redesigning and redeploying an entire process and all of its related services.

Rules engines have intuitive interfaces and approaches for designing business rules, including simple tables, graphical flow diagrams, and other complex visual decision trees and tools. After rules are defined, rule services are easily pushed to the ESB and can be used in any number of business processes. The process execution engine executes the rule services like any other ESB service.

The design of user interfaces

In a BPM environment, process workers manage and perform many day-to-day tasks by interfacing with computers running Web-based applications. BPM suites include an integrated capability to build the applications and their user interfaces (UIs). The ability to assemble process applications is often called a Composite Application Framework (CAF).

BPM CAF environments are fast and easy to use. The CAF employs a technique known as "codeless" application development for building and presenting the user interfaces to end users. It's called *codeless*, because the developer needn't write any computer code, such as Java or HTML, to build them. CAF tools employ the BPM drag-and-drop approach and incorporate the most advanced interface development tools.

CAF tools use Web 2.0 technologies like AJAX to deliver a rich experience to the user. The most advanced tools also have controls that can be dragged-and-dropped onto the design palette to rapidly build new forms and UIs. These tools typically have a WYSIWYG methodology where the actual screen that a user sees can be viewed at any time during development.

In BPM, you use one platform to design and build both processes and CAF user interfaces. Also, you can use third-party tools to build and run applications and connect them to the process execution engine with a Web service.

Simulation

After you design a process, you may want to first test it "in the lab." With BPM, you can computer-simulate a process to see how it will behave in a variety of conditions.

You simulate a process in the same environment used for modeling. Therefore, a simulation can be performed quickly. A process simulation is run as a project under one or more scenarios. A simulation project contains process simulation models, shared resources, and document configurations.

Simulations run processes through what-if scenarios while you adjust for changes in task characteristics such as resource requirements, cost, durations (cycle time), and queuing characteristics. The resources can be just about anything, such as machines, paper, partner services, manpower, parts, and so on and can be shared across one or more processes.

Because many processes are triggered by the arrival of a document, the creation of process instances for simulation is controlled through document generation. Document configurations define both arrival distributions and priorities. Simulation results are presented graphically, with information about completed work steps, queue lengths, incoming documents, document routing within the process, starting, stopping, and so on.

So how do you figure out what works and what doesn't? With reports! Simulations produce reports. Real-time reports provide immediate feedback, and are constantly updated as the simulation progresses. Analysts use these graphical reports to quickly determine the effects of the changes they've made in the simulation run. Post-simulation reports provide more detail, including simulation data, analytics, and charts.

Round-tripping in simulation — perhaps its most important feature — denotes using production data so that processes can be optimized and then implemented directly in the underlying process model.

The Execution Environment

The *execution environment* is the real-time operational system that manages and monitors processes as they perform.

Process execution engine

The execution engine orchestrates the activities and interactions of the process model. It handles the routing of work tasks to people, according to the routing rules defined in the model. It handles escalations and delegations and manages the state of the workflow — ensuring that work is completed. It coordinates interactions with third-party applications through the middleware and also provides process audits.

Analytics engine

The analytics engine is a very busy beaver during process execution. It collects and analyzes process data for presentation to process owners. Here are some of its tasks:

- **Process tracking:** Continuously collect and process data about the transactions connected to a process. Track volumes (such as number of loans processed or value of orders approved), velocities (cycle times, step completion times), errors (such as transactions occurring out of sequence), and special user-defined conditions.

- **Alerting:** Notify users whenever specific alert criteria are met or alert thresholds are exceeded. Delivers alerts via e-mail, mobile devices, or through Web services.

- **Statistical learning:** Build a knowledge base of performance statistics based on time-centric criteria, such as time-of-day or time-of-week. Automatically generate upper and lower statistical boundaries, based on historical patterns, for use by the alert engine.

- **Predictive analysis:** Based on volume and velocity data from both active processes and history, understand how the process is performing. Make statistically-valid predictions of future events. For example, detecting potential degradation scenarios, raising alerts, or taking action to correct the condition before service is impacted.

The Unified Workspace

The top layer in the BPM technology architecture is the *unified workspace*. This workspace is what the end user (the process worker) sees. It coordinates and facilitates day-to-day tasks, as specified by the process model.

Task inboxes

Task inboxes are the primary interface between the process execution environment and the process worker. Using e-mail or Web page notification, they alert the worker of tasks and present information on status, priority escalation, and delegation.

Process and people management

Process managers have their own ways to manage a process and the actions of the people who perform within it. Managers see a higher-level view of the tasks assigned out to process workers and their current state. They also have the ability to manually reallocate work as appropriate. In addition, best-of-breed BAM tools (see the "Monitoring dashboards" section for more information) deploy KPIs that allow these managers to view the performance of individual process workers and their effectiveness on particular tasks within the process.

With the rapid application-building capabilities in BPM technology, developers can build new user interfaces for people to interact with packaged applications. These user interfaces can either present data to users as part of their task execution or provide forms for the input of data connected to that task.

Monitoring dashboards

Business users can track the progress of operating processes using *Business Activity Monitoring* (BAM). With BAM, business users perform their own analysis and determine the root cause of process problems. BAM tools present information in a highly intuitive graphical manner. See Figure 5-4.

BAM tools present a user with a high-level visualization of an executing process, with clear indications of critical path flows and process bottlenecks. The user can drill down and explore levels of detail — by process step or by KPI rule — to determine where problems are occurring. BAM tools also provide additional analytical capabilities, such as the ability to correlate different KPIs and explore interactions.

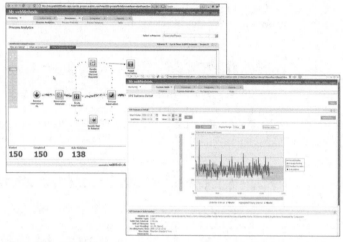

Figure 5-4: BAM displays.

Monitoring dashboards use the same precise visual depiction of the process model as was defined in the modeling tool at the commencement of the life-cycle. Business users see the operation of the same process they specified.

Third-Party Components

There's even more! BPM technology interfaces with a number of popular third-party tools — including Microsoft Office, Lotus Notes, ERP systems, Document Management Systems, analytical tools like Minitab, and Business Intelligence tools. With BPM you include these and other similar IT assets as part of the solution. BPM allows you to leverage most any tool to get the most out of your total IT investments.

Chapter 6

Getting There from Here

● ●

In This Chapter

▶ Recognizing the success criteria for implementing BPM

▶ Understanding various approaches for implementing BPM

▶ Developing a customized roadmap for implementing BPM

▶ Measuring the benefits of BPM

● ●

*B*PM is a comprehensive discipline that brings together process-centric thinking, process improvement methodologies, and key leading technologies to improve performance in response to business drivers and strategic imperatives. You can use BPM to:

✔ Forge a virtually integrated, global value chain that includes your customers, partners, and suppliers.

✔ Achieve cost efficiencies in commoditized markets.

✔ Improve the productivity of business operations.

✔ Position your company to innovate in products, services, processes, operations, and supply chains.

✔ Deliver value faster; become highly responsive.

✔ Ensure compliance with regulatory requirements and with internal management control mechanisms.

✔ Solve information overload problems; provide your business with the right information at the right time for decision-making.

✔ Facilitate communication and collaboration.

✔ Instill an unwavering focus on delivering customer value.

These paint an enticing picture of an attractive destination, but how do you get there? How do you implement BPM?

Laying the Foundation

BPM is not something you can achieve overnight. Instead, you must make the commitment to a long-term strategy. BPM will also pay short-term rewards and help you build on its successes. Technical implementation, performance improvement, and change management all play a part in the discipline of BPM. If you prepare for your journey by laying the foundation for each of these, you set the stage for near-term wins and long-term sustained success.

The strategic imperative

Chapter 2 lists many reasons to implement BPM, and most of them apply to everyone. But it's difficult to lead a charge and excite the masses with a laundry list. The most successful initiatives are launched and sustained with a core focus that can be articulated clearly and crystallized into messages that become deeply-rooted and highly personal for everyone in the organization. Ask the question, "Why are we doing this?"

Know your goals

Identify and articulate clearly the goals for process performance. Examine which KPIs reflect the condition of processes and the systems of management control. Focus on the critical few KPIs that give you the most leverage.

Follow a process methodology

A process methodology (such as Lean or Six Sigma) is critical to BPM success. Your business may have chosen a methodology already; if so, that's great. If not, you're best served to pick one or develop something new. This way, you have a sufficient basis for deploying BPM technology and you will accelerate the gains in business performance.

Include the IT staff in process methodology training.

Set up the architectures

BPM has three dimensions to it. You must set up the architectures for each.

- ✔ **Business and management architectures:** Put in place the systems and procedures for managing change, projects, and programs. Identify the key stakeholders, and plan for managing their involvement and support. Chapter 4 describes how to make this happen.

- ✔ **Deploy the process architecture:** Because you're moving toward a process-centric business structure, you must set up your process architecture. Define the roles of process owners and cross-functional process teams. Conduct process training. Instill process governance. Implement process-centric business operations.

  Create a BPM Center of Excellence to institutionalize process architecture within your company.

- ✔ **The technology architecture:** Deploy an integrated BPM suite on a sound technology architecture. Include the tools and techniques for modeling, analysis, simulation, rules, metadata, SOA governance, design, workflow, development, and deployment. Chapter 5 describes the technology architecture of BPM.

  Set up an Integration Competency Center.

Define measurement systems

You only know how well any initiative affects the business if you have a good system of measurement. The first technical activity in BPM is to implement the monitoring and management of selected core and enabling processes. Measurements lead directly to improvements and fuel early success and momentum.

Preparing for the Bigger Issues

BPM will affect your entire enterprise. Consider making some adjustments as you go forward.

Many analyst and consulting firms have process capability and maturity models, and can help you set up an assessment.

Making BPM an effective enterprise-wide business transformation program requires that you understand the following:

✔ **Corporate culture:** The culture of your company influences adoption of BPM. If your company is entrepreneurial, consider starting with a project that quickly proves BPM's value and buys you the political capital to expand its footprint within your company. Alternately, you may have a methodical, strategic, and consensus-building culture in your company. In this case, you should plan on a long cycle of building awareness, education, and planning. Include in your team people responsible for enterprise planning and architecture.

✔ **Risk attitude:** In BPM, risk comes from poor preparation. Once you have your business, process, management, and technical architectures in place, the risks of implementing any given project are small. Conversely, risk increases as elements of the architectures go missing. Be sure to implement the financial measures so you can evaluate and demonstrate the ROI.

✔ **The IT environment:** Corporate IT environments seem to have a little of everything — from legacy and antiquated systems to home-grown systems, and of course modern architectural elements, with SOA and even Web 2.0. The more your environment is biased toward legacy systems, the more important the middleware and metadata architecture. At the same time, this bias provides more opportunity to showcase re-use!

✔ **Professional development:** BPM proficiency requires new skills. These can be gained through professional training and development. If you already have a CPI program in place, you'll be able to leverage the knowledge and expertise in process thinking, process modeling, analysis, and optimization. Otherwise, you'll need to roll out a training program on process-centricity. Appendix B has references for process education.

Failure to train in process concepts leads to program failures.

Taking Your First Steps

Once you're ready, where do you begin with BPM? Take your first steps in areas that can return value quickly — in a matter of a few months at the most. Select projects that influence core processes and return the highest customer value, as opposed to indirect, enabling processes. And don't be afraid to jump right in. BPM projects come in two flavors:

- ✔ **Optimize current operations:** Improve productivity and performance by measuring current operating processes and correcting defects. Using BAM, monitor and analyze processes, and determine areas for improvement.

- ✔ **Develop new processes and applications:** Pursue growth and innovation, or eliminate wasteful practices, by building new capabilities. Use BPM's integrated composition environment to reuse existing capabilities, compose new processes, and deploy them.

BPM implementations can work within nearly any development methodology. Be sure to have support from process owners, and handle exceptions in your manual processes. During user acceptance testing, use process models to describe to users how their lives change as a result of a BPM initiative.

Phased delivery is best suited for BPM projects so that you can demonstrate quick ROI, get support, and mitigate risk of project failure. This can be incremental or layered. In the incremental approach, you optimize and automate complete sub-processes in each phase. In the layered approach, you optimize and automate selected process steps in each phase.

Showing Them the Money

You now know that BPM addresses the business needs of your company and extends business processes to your customers, partners, and suppliers.

Achieving ROI

With BPM, you build and deploy new capabilities that create new value and lower costs, time spent, and waste. All this spells positive Return on Investment (ROI). In addition, you build these new capabilities faster, at a lower cost, and with more leverage — all of which contribute to even greater ROI.

If you use a program like Six Sigma, you already measure project value creation. BPM dovetails directly into such programs, and is naturally part of the ROI equation.

BPM eliminates mundane, non-value-added tasks. You focus your people on those activities that only people do best: analysis, decision-making, and innovation. Such increased attention to key business drivers yields significant ROI.

Benefits for constituencies

Remember that with BPM, everyone benefits. Be sure to measure and recognize the value created for each of your constituencies. Business users benefit from new visibility and metrics, faster time to new capabilities, eliminating non-value-added work; and gaining agility, flexibility, and self-sufficiency. Information technologists benefit from meeting business needs quickly — being off the critical path, reusing IT assets, scaling, achieving lower costs, and spending more time in development and less in support. Customers, partners, and suppliers gain improved customer service and satisfaction, value-stream alignment, faster response — and in general, making you easier to do business with!

Obliterate the gaps!

BPM removes not only the gap between IT and business groups, but also gaps between all business functions. Teams communicate more seamlessly and effectively, shed mundane and non-value-added work, operate more strategically, and adapt faster to change.

Chapter 7

Ten Best Practices of BPM

*K*eep these ten things in mind and you'll be well on your way to BPM success:

✔ **Think process; be process.** Set a cross-functional organization in place to drive and sustain your process orientation. Process teams and process owners should plan together, meet regularly, and work collaboratively. Be certain that the main stakeholder is directly involved.

✔ **Get smart!** BPM is a new discipline and the skills can be hard to come by. But the people around you have most of what you need. They may not have the job titles, but they'll have the right understanding of your business, the people, the processes, and the right raw skills to be successful. Train them! Appeal to service providers for help, especially in the short term as you gear up. And, believe it or not, you're not going to learn quite everything from this book! Get out and see what people are doing. Attend a conference, visit Web sites, read blogs. Seek out companies that have done this before — and created real business value.

✔ **Adopt an executive.** Find the senior-most individuals whose responsibility is to solve the big problems and enlist them as sponsors, advocates, and evangelists. Get them excited and educated about what BPM can do for them. Show them a demonstration of what's possible and they'll jump on board.

✔ **Great expectations.** BPM programs involve many stakeholders, and each will naturally form his own perspectives and definitions of success. Be clear about the value proposition of your programs and projects. Repeat these often, and deliver on them directly, avoiding "expectation creep."

✔ **Pick a methodology.** Do you already have a process improvement program like Lean or Six Sigma in your company? If so, these are an effective foundation for BPM. If not, pick something. Select the process improvement and management methodology that's right for you, and set this in place as a cornerstone of your process architecture.

✔ **The right technology.** Do your homework and choose technology that best fills your needs and requirements. The technology varies considerably from vendor to vendor. After finding a technology set that fits your architecture, be sure to run it through its paces: ask for custom demonstrations and make sure the vendor shows you what it can do.

✔ **Hear the voice of the customer.** The point of BPM is to create customer value. Use BPM to see your business the way your customers do. Your customers don't care how things get done, they only care that they experience exceptional service and receive what they ordered — at the best price, and when they wanted it. Remember that everything you're doing should ultimately create more value for your customers.

✔ **Pick a project.** So many processes, so little time! How do you choose? Select the project that provides the greatest return to your business and can be completed in three months or less. And remember, you don't have to improve entire processes all at once.

✔ **Measure first.** Don't start designing new processes until you understand what's happening with your current ones. You wouldn't let a doctor administer treatment without a thorough diagnosis would you? So don't start implementing process change until you have diagnosed their current state. Using BAM, establish the baseline metrics. Only then are you operating from a position of knowledge.

✔ **Plan to change.** BPM is a change system. It's designed to help you identify where change is needed and for you to make changes quickly and get to the next level of operational performance. With such a powerful toolset, you need to surround BPM with support for change. Manage change, implement policies for making changes, articulate change approvals, recognize change events, measure change, reward change.

Chapter 8

Ten BPM Pitfalls to Avoid

In This Chapter
▶ Avoiding the most common mistakes
▶ Increasing your chances of success

*P*ay attention to these warning signs and you can avoid making BPM mistakes:

✔ **Firing too early.** BPM technology tempts you with its promises of visibility, productivity, and fast results. You might be seduced into plowing ahead without methodology, architecture, and process. This is a shortcut to failure. Take the time to get the business, process, and management dimensions of BPM in place before you attack the technology.

✔ **Thinking in stovepipes.** Don't think functionally! Process-centric thinking is different. Cross-functional solutions are different. You need to be thinking end-to-end; about how a value-chain comes together; how your role, performance, and productivity create value within the greater process. Getting everyone to think this way takes time and persistence.

If you put a process-centric model in place, but leave the incentives and controls in the hands of functional owners, your initiative will wander off course. Processes should be owned by process owners.

✔ **Making a RIF program.** If you make BPM a veiled headcount reduction initiative, you will guarantee failure. People make processes work, and if you use a process initiative to justify a Reduction-In-Force (RIF) initiative, the program will die. BPM is for helping people work more effectively and generate more value. If workers re-engineer a process to work themselves out of a job, retrain and relocate them. And do so with great fanfare!

✔ **Solving problems once.** Don't just train an implementation team on how to do a one-time solution. Seek out training and professional development that will "teach them to fish." Be sure to figure out how to facilitate continuous and sustaining change. Be sure to include senior executives, IT staff, and users.

✔ **Not supporting users.** BPM empowers process owners and participants to implement change. Be sure you support them with the policies, authority, rewards and recognition, compensation, and other means of facilitation. In particular, BPM empowers business users in ways that require the IT systems to share responsibility. Don't overlook the need to make this happen.

✔ **Ignoring the end users.** Don't overfund infrastructure at the expense of the process participants: the end-users. Treat the users like customers; make them more productive and the technology more invisible, so their day-to-day tasks can continually add more value.

✔ **Forgetting to celebrate.** Rolling out something in three months that used to take two years is worth celebrating. Achieving a lofty business goal for productivity or customer satisfaction is worth celebrating. BPM projects may be shorter and the improvements more incremental, but you must measure and celebrate the successes.

✔ **Hard-wiring the framework.** BPM was created to help you create adaptive processes. But you have to design for flexibility. Don't just hard-wire today's answer at the expense of building in the flexibility to ensure that the answer can change to be effective in tomorrow's world.

✔ **Using "gut feel."** BPM provides the visibility and measures for fact-based decision-making. If you don't let the data drive decisions, and if you fall back and let intuition and tradition drive your decisions, you will be squandering your investment and your opportunities.

✔ **Automating failure.** Chinese proverb says, "Man who shoots self in foot should not buy automatic weapon." If a process is broken, then automating it will only generate errors faster. Because BPM enables an unprecedented level of automation in actions, activities, and decisions, this doesn't mean you just start automating things. BPM provides you the methods and tools to analyze and improve processes, and then automate them when they're performing optimally.

Appendix A

Glossary

· ·

Asynchronous Java and XML (AJAX): A Web development technique that makes Web pages more responsive by exchanging small amounts of data so that the entire Web page doesn't have to reload each time the user requests a change.

Balance Scorecard: A framework for identifying business metrics beyond the basic financial measures normally used. Balance Scorecards include customer, process, and people measures as well as financial information, and ties together strategic goals with operational metrics.

BPM Suite (BPMS): A comprehensive software set facilitating all aspects of business process management, including process design, workflow, applications, integration, and activity monitoring for both system and human-centric environments.

Business Activity Monitoring (BAM): Software for the real-time monitoring of business processes.

Business Process Execution Language (BPEL): A serialized XML programming language for the specification of executable business processes, applied primarily to the orchestration of Web services.

Business Process Management (BPM): The methods, techniques, and tools used to design, enact, control, and analyze operational business processes involving people, systems, applications, data, and organizations.

Business Process Modeling Notation (BPMN): A standardized graphical notation for drawing business processes in a workflow, facilitating improved communication and portability of process models.

Business Rules: The formal codification of business policies and actions into prescriptive operational practices that are externalized from and maintained independently of application code.

Business Transformation: A programmatic business initiative that realigns people, process, and technology to achieve significant changes and improvements in performance.

Business Visibility: Tools and techniques that provide real-time visibility and insight into business activities and processes.

Codeless Application Development: Tools and techniques to assemble code components, services, and controls, as well as frameworks for building new applications using wizards and forms.

Composite Application Frameworks (CAF): A software structure for developing applications and user interfaces based on the modular reuse and composition of services, logic, user interface components, and business processes.

Continuous Process Improvement (CPI): An unceasing effort to discover and eliminate the causes of problems in the performance of business processes and increase value creation and productivity.

Cycle Time: The total elapsed time from the time a task, product, or service is started until it is completed.

Dashboard: A visual display that indicates the status or health of a business enterprise or process via numeric and graphical key performance indicators.

Delivered In-Full and On-Time (DIFOT): A key measure of supply chain performance, which measures how often the customer gets what they want when they want it.

DMAIC: The acronym for the five core phases of the Six Sigma methodology: Define, Measure, Analyze, Improve, Control; used to solve process and business problems through data and analytical methods.

Enterprise Application Integration (EAI): The tools and practice of linking computer applications and data together in order to achieve operational and business advantages.

Enterprise Service Bus (ESB): Part of the category of middleware infrastructure, an ESB is a software architecture construct that provides foundational services for information systems via an event-driven messaging engine.

Governance: A framework for decision and accountability that produces desirable outcomes within the organization. The governance framework determines the what, who, and how of enterprise decision-making.

Helga: The omnipresent force of BPM.

Integrated Composition Environment (ICE): A services-based and model-driven toolset for the collaborative assembly of loosely-coupled, business-oriented, and results-driven process applications.

Key Performance Indicators (KPIs): Any set of financial or non-financial metrics that can be measured to quantify business performance. For example, process cycle time.

Lean: An improvement methodology based on a customer-centric definition of value, and providing that value in the most effective way possible, through a combination of the elimination of waste and a motivated and engaged workforce.

Measure First: The practice of beginning a BPM project or initiative by first measuring the present state of a business process to establish a valid baseline.

Orchestration: The automated arrangement, coordination, execution, and management of complex computer applications, systems, integration, and services.

Performance Optimization: The practice of making adjustments and changes to business activities and processes in order to improve performance.

Portal: A software framework that enables people, via a unitary interface provided through a Web browser, to manage information and processes across systems or organizations.

Predictive Analytics: Algorithms applied to patterns of information about activities and behaviors that serve as a statistically-valid basis for predicting potential future outcomes.

Process: A set of activities, material, and/or information flow that transforms a set of inputs into defined outputs.

Process Framework: The architecture of an extended process or set of processes that enables a set of business functionality.

Process Model: A representative prescription for how a set of activities should operate in a flow and sequence in order to regularly achieve desired outcomes.

Process Optimization: The practice of making changes and adjustments to a process in order to improve its efficiency or effectiveness.

Process Owner: The individual who has responsibility for process performance and resources, and who provides support, resources, and functional expertise to projects.

The process owner is accountable for implementing process improvements.

Service-Oriented Architecture: A software architecture where both new and existing functionalities are packaged and provided as services.

Simulation: The computer modeling of a hypothetical situation that can be analyzed to determine how a given application of systems may operate when deployed.

Six Sigma: A proven and proscriptive set of analytical tools, project control techniques, reporting methods, and management techniques that combine to form breakthrough improvements in problem-solving and business performance.

Supply Chain: The system of people, activities, information, and resources involved in the movement of a product or service from supplier to customer.

Total Quality Management (TQM): A management strategy that embeds the awareness of quality into all organizational structures and processes.

Value Stream: The flow of materials and information through a process to deliver a product or service to a customer.

Voice of the Customer (VOC): The representation of the expressed and unexpressed needs, wants, and desires of the recipient of a process output, a product, or a service; usually expressed as a specification, requirements or expectations.

Web Service Definition Language (WSDL): WSDL is an XML format for describing network services as a set of endpoints operating on messages containing either document-oriented or procedure-oriented information.

XML Process Definition Language (XPDL): an XML-based process definition language to allow process models to be consistently represented and edited across process modeling tools.

Workflow: An orchestrated and repeatable pattern of business activity enabled by the systematic organization of resources into processes that transform materials, provide services, or process information.

WYMIWYR: "What You Model Is What You Run": An acronym that captures how a fully integrated BPMS connects modeling to the runtime environment.

Appendix B

Resources

● ●

Web Resources

- ✔ `bpTrends.com` provides whitepapers and articles from gurus as well as its own reports on BPM vendors.

- ✔ `eBizQ.net` is a good source for both BPM and SOA.

- ✔ `bpminstitute.org` offers reviews, articles, Webinars and online resources — a very extensive site!

- ✔ `bpmi.org` is a good site that focuses more on standards and less on technology.

- ✔ `bpm.com` is a good mix of thought leadership and vendor-provided content.

- ✔ `alignjournal.com` is a great resource for those more interested in the business side of BPM.

Blogs

- ✔ Sandy Kemsley's BPM blog (`www.Column2.com`): Sandy, an independent BPM expert, blogs almost daily.

- ✔ Bruce Silver's BPMS Watch (`http://69.36.189.101/wordpress`): Bruce also provides reviews and reports on various BPM technology vendors.

- ✔ Co-author Kiran Garimella maintains two entertaining BPM blogs: `www.bpmenterprise.com/blog/index.asp?ui=Kiran%20Garimella&s=bloggers` and `www.ebizq.net/blogs/bpmblog/`.

Books

✔ *Business Process Management: The Third Wave* by Howard Smith and Peter Fingar (Meghan Kiffer Pr).

✔ *Business Process Management: Profiting From Process* by Roger Burlton (Sams).

✔ *Business Process Change, Second Edition: A Guide for Business Managers*, by Paul Harmon (Morgan Kaufmann).

✔ *The Power of Process: Unleashing the Source of Competitive Advantage* by Kiran K. Garimella (Meghan Kiffer Pr).

To find more books on BPM, go to www.mkpress.com.

Conferences

✔ **Shared Insights & IIR BPM Conference** (www.iirusa.com): A focus on the practical aspects of implementing BPM; good for business analysts and project leaders.

✔ **Gartner BPM Summit** (www.gartner.com): See thought leaders, customers, and vendors; good for architects and business leaders.

✔ **Forrester Technology Leadership Forum** (www.forrester.com): See experts, case studies, and technologies in one location. Good conference for all roles in the BPM initiative; a focus on strategy.

✔ **ISSSP Leadership Conference** (Six Sigma) (www.ISSSP.com): A focus on success stories and practical advice on continuous process improvement.

Technology Vendors

Vendors have great knowledge and expertise. Of course each has a perspective that's in their own self-interest, but they're betting their business on understanding what's right for the marketplace. They want you to be informed and will spend marketing and sales money informing you.

Consultancies and Integrators

Every major systems integrator now has a BPM practice with breadth of experience in implementing business solutions using BPM methods and technologies, and are well versed in assisting with the cultural and organizational challenges. Many regional and boutique firms specialize in areas around BPM, such as process methodologies, modeling, development, applications, integration, operations, and more. Some will specialize in a particular market or industry.

Analyst Firms

- ✔ Gartner Research (www.gartner.com): Covers a broad range of products and methodologies, along with an annual review of the vendor landscape.

- ✔ Forrester Research (www.forrester.com): Provides research on vendors and events on best practices, as well as annual reports on the top BPM vendors.

- ✔ AMR (www.amrresearch.com): In-depth research and focused events on both SOA and BPM.

- ✔ Burton Group (www.burtongroup.com): Provides strong technical research and advisory services.

- ✔ Macehiter Ward-Dutton (www.mwdadvisors.com): Specifically focuses on IT-Business alignment.

- ✔ Aberdeen (www.aberdeen.com): Go to Aberdeen for online technical advisory materials and fact-based research studies.

- ✔ Current Analysis (www.currentlanalysis.com): Offers a broad range of industry and technology research.

Training and Education

- ✔ BPtrends (www.bptrends.com)
- ✔ The Association of Business Process Professionals (www.abpmp.com)
- ✔ Process Renewal Group (www.processrenewal.com)

Look Around You!

You have more resources than you may realize. Your co-workers may have experience in Six Sigma, Lean, or have worked in matrixed environments. You have business people in your IT organization, and IT people in your business organization. You have champions and supporters of change and young people aggressively pursuing new approaches. Take advantage of your own network of experience and support.

Software AG

Software AG (www.softwareag.com) is the world's largest independent provider of business infrastructure software, delivering best-in-class BPM solutions. Software AG brings you education, training, references, resources, world-class partners and consultants, and a fully-integrated BPM Suite.